Human Geography

Gilbert McInnis

In Exile Publications

Halifax, Canada

National Library of Canada Cataloguing
in Publication
McInnis, Gilbert (1963-)

Copyright © 2014 by Gilbert McInnis

ISBN:978-0-9876759-4-1

© Gilbert McInnis 1999 Library of Congress
Washington D.C.

Canadian Drama, Literature, Science Fiction.

.

Typesetting & Cover Design: InExile Design
Contact InExile at inexilepublications@gmail.com

Human Geography was first produced on January 15, 16, and 17, 1999, at Theatre de poche, Universitè Laval, Quebec.

ORIGINAL CAST

Blake	Eric Brüshett
Sandra/Vala	Julie Labrie
Dr.Frazer	Louis H. Campagna
Dr. Skinner	Larry Hodgson

CREW

Producer	Gib McInnis
Director	Gib McInnis
Set Design	Yan Courtois
	Cheryl Rimmer
Prop Manger	Marie-Cecile Baspeyre
Makeup	Marie-Cecile Baspeyre
	Eric Brüshett
Publicity	Johanne Jobin
Program/Posters	Paul Gosslin

NOTES FROM THE AUTHOR

I was inspired to write *Human Geography* essentially because of two works, *The Abolition of Man*, written by C.S. Lewis, and a later book written by Francis Schaeffer, *Back to Freedom and Dignity*. Both works examine the changes happening to our human dignity within a context of revolutionary change; a society moving away from a democracy towards a soft-totalitarian society of the posthuman. As we draw closer to fulfilling a theoretical definition of totalitarianism, by our pursuit of building a posthuman society, I feel we will be faced with an entirely different human struggle as never before. Our struggle will be to assert our humanness while being persuaded we are nothing else than super-animal types. We may adapt to this posthuman environment marginally, but a meaningful life is always achieved in a pursuit of our *personelness*.

In this revolutionary context, *Human Geography* perhaps is a microcosm for something much larger being "Mapped" out in our society; a conquest is underway for our humanity. If humans are only to be considered as super-animal types, as the elite technocrats would have us believe, then it is logical that with each new territory gained over our "human geography" humans will move away from this "personelness" toward the posthuman. Therefore, we should not let ourselves be "reduced" to mere genetic constructs by any impersonal godlike machine. I believe we can retain our human dignity if we will assert what makes us human: spirit, soul, and flesh. To ignore this "trinity" is to reject who we are. So, I wrote this play as an assertion of our human dignity.

The play has four roles, one female, and three males. The female role has to play two characters, Sandra and Vala, since they are of one body. The setting is present or near future, and the questions raised by the play make it a science-fiction play. In fact, I believe my play maybe the first science fiction play written in Canada. However, the themes of the play do not rely heavily on sci-fi. I have explained the play as a genetically designed love dilemma.

The whole play takes place in Walden, which is a research center founded by Dr. Skinner. Dr. Skinner is a genetic engineer (instead of a behaviouralist), and Dr. Skinner operates his research center with the help of human clients who donate their body fluids (mostly sperm and ovum). In this way, the humans can stay at Walden free of charge. Because Walden is supported by the sale of human body fluids, there are certain rules that must be respected; one is no pregnancy or child rearing. But, human love upsets this rule.

Sandra/Vala is a character who is a recent participant at Walden. She has made a deal with Dr. Skinner to stay there. If she provides ovum for his project, he is supposed to help her get rid of her second personality, Vala. However, while staying at Walden, Sandra and Vala fall in love with another resident, Blake; a resident who has been engineered by a human. Blake is supposed to be genetically perfect. However, he does not get along that well with Sandra's other side, Vala. After becoming pregnant, Sandra is ordered to leave, but at the dismay of Vala, since Vala is dependent on Walden for all her needs and desires. In the end their will to exercise their humanity to its fullest becomes a guiding light in their universal quest for individual and communal love.

Gib McInnis

CHARACTERS

Blake	A mature teenager.
Sandra	A young lady in love with Blake. She has a second younger personality, Vala. Vala desires Blake, but Blake is indifferent to her.
Dr. Skinner	A genetic engineer and founder of Walden; he is about fifty-five years old.
Frazer	An intern doctor at Walden. He is somewhat naive and at times comic.

ACT ONE

Scene 1

A computer is raised in the center of the stage like an alter. The screen is illuminated as if it is alive with light. Blake and Vala enter. Vala is following Blake with a bottle in her hand.

Vala   Come on Blake, party with me. Don't let me drink this by myself.

Blake   Leave me alone Vala.

Vala   Why?

Blake   Because you'll end up doing something terrible, like last time—or worse!

Vala   If I was Sandra you wouldn't dick me off like this. I'm sure you'd suck up to me like a little baby.

Blake   Stop it! You're so vulgar, not like Sandra.

Vala   I can fake her if you like.

Laughing as she takes a drink.

Blake   No you can't, and anyway she hates alcohol.

Vala   No she doesn't, she's just scared of what it will do to her. Screw her! I'll drink for the both of us. (Giving him the bottle) Here, try some?

Blake   What is it?

Vala   It's wine.

Blake   It doesn't smell like wine.

Vala   Oh, you're very smart. That's because I added something special to it.

Blake   I'm not drinking anything of yours again.

Vala   I was trying to be nice to you. Try it.

3

Blake	Thanks, but no thanks!
Vala	(Taking an apple out of her pocket) Well, here then, I brought you this (She tosses him an apple), since you're always hungry.
Blake	I'm sorry, I didn't mean to be so mean to you.

He goes to bite into it, then smells it.

Vala	What's wrong, don't you like it?
Blake	Yes, but it's just that I feel a little funny about this, that's all. (He sees a hole in the apple) Where did you get it?
Vala	I took it from one of the trees in Skinner's garden.
Blake	You sure you didn't find it on the ground?
Vala	No! I plucked it off the tree myself.
Blake	(Looking at closely) You did something to it, didn't you?
Vala	Oh come on Blake—you're paranoid. Go ahead— eat it.
Blake	You're lying, it smells like...(He smells it again, then approaches her and holds her) What did you do to it? You'd better tell me the truth now!
Vala	Leave me alone, get your fucking hands off of me.
Blake	You're trying to trick me again, aren't you? (Taking her by the arm) Aren't you?
Vala	All right, all right, I spiked it with methadone, now let me go.
Blake	Where did you get the methadone from?
Vale	I borrowed it from a cabinet in Skinner's office.
Blake	You know he'll find out sooner or later.

Vala	He's got lots. Anyway, I added some water to the bottle, so he won't miss it at all. I put some in the wine too. Go on have a drink. It's pretty good, you get a buzz of it in about fifteen minutes.
Blake	No. It's against rules.
Vala	Fuck Skinner's rules! Let's have a little fun?
Blake	No Vala. I know what you're up to this time.
Vala	Come on just one. I don't want to drink this alone.
Blake	(Taking the bottle) You drank all this?
Vala	There's some left for you, drink it?
Blake	No! I should pour it out.
Vala	No, give it to me, I'll finish it.
Blake	You have to finish it, don't you?
Vala	Yes—the sooner the better.
Blake	You'll end up killing yourself if you keep dumping garbage like this down your throat.
Vala	I really don't care for your moralizing—it's kind of negative—if you don't mind.
Blake	Then stop drinking it now!
Vala	Like my life, when I finish it, I'll stop.
Blake	Well I'm glad to see you have a limit.
Vala	I don't have limits, I've learned to live around them.
Blake	You're getting smashed!
Vala	(Angry) I'm tired of you smashing me out like a cigarette. Fuck your limits. That's your problem, you have too many god dam limits. (Taking the bottle while he is holding onto it) Pour it into me.

(He embraces her to get the bottle. She laughs now) You can pour all you want into me, Blake. Oh, now I got you, come on.

She tries to kiss him, but he avoids her.

Blake Don't ever come near me again.

Vala You don't want me because I'm not like you?

Blake What do you mean?

Vala I heard Dr. Skinner tell Mr. Frazer, when he arrived, that you're supposed to be a perfect (She is stumbling to pronounce) speci...men.

Blake Specimen.

Vala I know!

Blake What else did they say about me?

Vala Skinner told Frazer that you have no parents. I can't figure it out, how did you pop into this fucking world then?

Blake I didn't pop into this world, I was incubated.

Vala You were what?

Blake I was created in a test-tube with a sperm and an ovum.

Vala Without any sex going on?

Blake Yes.

Vala They can do that.

Blake Don't you think that's redundant.

Vala Not really, I think.

Blake Of course it is—stupid—here I am in front of you.

Vala They created you without having any sex?

Blake	Yes.
Vala	That's really sad.
Blake	Why?
Vala	They've taken all the fun out of it.
Blake	It wasn't supposed to be fun; it was supposed to be for an experiment.
Vala	But you must have parents somewhere?
Blake	Yes, but I really don't know who they are. Dr. Skinner said my biological ancestors wanted it that way.
Vala	So you don't know who they are?
Blake	I know one of them won a Noble prize for physics and the other has a Ph.D.
Vala	Is that good?
Blake	Of course it is, for me that is.
Vala	Well, we have something in common.
Blake	Like what?
Vala	I don't know who my parents are either.
Blake	Why not?
Vala	They left us in an orphanage when we were young. I guess they couldn't handle the both of us all at once.
Blake	And either can I.
Vala	Will you stop putting me down.
Blake	All right. I'll stop.
Vala	But can you have sex with another person, I mean who isn't created like you, and everything will be okay afterwards for her?

Blake   Of course I can.

Vala   But you can't love anyone the same way, is that it?

Blake   No. I can.

Vala   Then why don't you love me?

Blake   Because I love Sandra instead.

Vala   No you don't love her. You just want to have sex with her, that's all.

Blake   You don't see any difference do you?

Vala   Yes. I do. Have sex with me, and you'll see the difference.

Blake   No, I can't.

Vala   Oh come on.

Blake   No, and stop annoying me.

Vala   Well, just give me a kiss then?

Blake   No, I made a promise to Sandra that I'd never to touch you again.

Vala   Look, I'll screw your brains out more than she'll ever. She doesn't even like sex, but I do. No, I don't like it, I love it. Come on, Blake don't you want to have sex with someone who wants it as much as you do?

Blake   (Tempted) Leave me alone.

Vala   How could you enjoy sex with her, knowing that she really doesn't even like it. You did have sex with her—I know it.

Blake   You don't know anything.

Vala   You're lying.

Blake   I am not.

Vala	I know you banged her!
Blake	I didn't.
Vala	Then what about the last time we were alone?
Blake	Nothing happened.
Vala	We were both naked, when I left.
Blake	Sandra got dressed. You know how she is...
Vala	Oh, I know how she is, but I don't believe you.
Blake	You're were drunk, how would you know?
Vala	You're lying.
Blake	Do you think she would sleep with me? Think about that?
Vala	Maybe you're right. But why did she skip her period again?
Blake	She did?
Vala	It's six weeks late.
Blake	How are you so sure?
Vala	We share the same bathroom.
Blake	She's missed her period before.
Vala	Oh, now you're playing Dr. Blake.
Blake	I've noticed it before, that's all.
Vala	Well, well, I find it very interesting that you keep track of her period.
Blake	I'm not keeping track of nothing.
Vala	Tell me the truth. I know you slept with her, and you didn't even protect yourself.
Blake	How are you so sure?

Vala	Well, it's obvious, if she can't have her period, then you've got her knocked up, and if you've got her knocked up, then you didn't protect yourself.
Blake	You think you've got this all figured out, haven't you?
Vala	Skinner will figure it all out when I tell him.
Blake	You better keep your mouth shut.
Vala	Then, you'd better tell me the truth, now.
Blake	All right...you're right.
Vala	You fucked her! I knew it.
Blake	Love, Vala, love, don't you see that?
Vala	What ever, it doesn't matter what it is—if you get her knocked up—Skinner won't allow you to have the baby here. You know the rules.
Blake	If she's pregnant.
Vala	Six weeks late—probably she is.
Blake	He can allow us to stay, if he wanted to.
Vala	You know the first commandment around here, protect yourself. They keep shoving that rule down my throat. She'll be kicked out if they find out that you've broken the golden rule.
Blake	Then we'll leave.
Vala	No you won't!
Blake	Yes we will!
Vala	I don't want you to leave.
Blake	You'll leave too.
Vala	Let me talk to Dr Skinner first…
Blake	You'd better keep your mouth shut.

Vala	I might.
Blake	What do you mean by that?
Vala	It depends on how nice you're going to be with me.
Blake	You little...
Vala	Now, now, be nice or I'll tell.
Blake	What do you want?
Vala	A big fucking kiss.
Blake	No! I promised Sandra I wouldn't touch you again.
Vala	(Leaving) Well, I'll tell Skinner then.
Blake	(Taking her by the arm) Wait a minute. You're not really going to tell him, are you?
Vala	I'm waiting.
Blake	You promise you won't tell?
Vala	No—if you kiss me. But, if she's pregnant, he's going to find out sooner or later.
Blake	How are you so sure she's pregnant?
Vale	I just feel things, and I feel you are in shit!
Blake	If I kiss you, you'll keep your mouth shut until I find out for sure.
Vala	(Facing him ready for the kiss) Yes, but it depends how passionate the kiss is?
Blake	(Slowly moves to her then stops) I don't want to.
Vala	Why not?
Blake	I promised her that I wouldn't touch you.
Vala	Well, imagine that I'm her, and that these lips are hers.

Blake	You're too drunk!
Vala	Go for it. I couldn't care less how I get you to kiss me, just do it, now!

As Blake moves closer she grabs him.

Vala	Not so fast, let me enjoy it would you? (She embraces him) Now, that wasn't so hard was it?
Blake	But...
Vala	Who cares, just keep on cruising.
Blake	But I don't love you.
Vala	Then think of her while you give me another.
Blake	I can't believe I am doing this.
Vala	I don't care. Fake it until you make it!
Blake	But you're not Sandra.
Vala	Think harder. I'll try and help you. (Imitating Sandra) I enjoyed our night together Blake.
Blake	Stop it!
Vala	Enjoy me. She's enjoying it.
Blake	You think so?
Vala	Yes, I can feel it.
Blake	You can?
Vala	I can.
Blake	But she felt a little uncomfortable about it afterwards.
Vala	Well, I feel great about it now, and I'm enjoying it very much.
Blake	You are?
Vala	Yes. Totally!

Blake   Oh how I wish Sandra...(Frazer arrives then Blake stops) would feel this way.

Vala   She doesn't have to, I do.

Blake   Frazer's here. Stop it!

Vala   Who cares.

Blake   (Pushing her away) Stop it!

Vala   How come you won't cruise me? You cruised her.

Blake   Shut up! You said you'd keep your mouth shut.

Frazer Sandra?

Blake   It's Vala—not Sandra.

Frazer Vala, leave us alone, I've got to test Blake.

Blake   Sorry Fraz I didn't mean for this to happen. I tried to come here alone, but she followed me.

Vala   Why did you have to bother us?

Frazer Blake has to be tested.

Vala   He was being tested, and I wasn't finished either. Thanks to you.

Frazer Leave us alone Vala.

Vala   Can't I stick around to watch?

Blake   No.

Vala   I won't bother you.

Frazer Perhaps you would like me to modify your Lithium dosage, it'll just take one short behavioral report?

Vala   I'll leave when I want to.

Frazer Or maybe you would like to donate some more of your body fluids right now?

Vala	No thank you, I've had of enough of you poking around my body today.
Frazer	Then leave.
Vala	(She picks up the bottle) I'll finish this alone—bye Blake.

Scene 2

Frazer	I don't mean to pry, but did I hear Vala correctly?
Blake	About what?
Frazer	You seem to be intimately involved with Sandra?
Blake	I guess you heard enough?
Frazer	Yes.
Blake	Does it bother you?
Frazer	It's kind of contradictory—isn't it?
Blake	Why?
Frazer	Because she's been quite strict about being chaste.
Blake	Don't judge her Fraz—you don't know the whole story yet.
Frazer	All right, But did your exchange happen about six weeks ago?
Blake	Yeah, how did you calculate that?
Frazer	An educated guess. You're supposed to protect yourself when an incident like that happens, you know?
Blake	I did, I mean we did.
Frazer	You did for sure?
Blake	Yeah, I'm sure.

Frazer	If Dr. Skinner discovered that she was pregnant, he would enforce Walden's rule.
Blake	What do you think he'd do to us?
Frazer	If she decided to carry it to term, she'd have to leave Walden.
Blake	He could make an exception couldn't he?
Frazer	But that would make it very difficult for him to extract any ovum from her during the pregnancy and he would have to replace her with another patient. And besides, having a child around here would break his number one rule.
Blake	Why can't we change that rule—that seems to be easy to do around here?
Frazer	The rules of Walden must be respected if you want to live here freely. She'd have to leave or else?
Blake	Or else what?
Frazer	Or else she'd have to part with it.
Blake	You mean our child?
Frazer	I meant the embryo.
Blake	Oh. (Thinking) I don't believe Sandra would choose that.
Frazer	Then, you'd better prepare yourself for her departure.
Blake	I'd leave with her, and I don't think Dr. Skinner would want that, would he?
Frazer	Don't you think he might have already considered that?
Blake	No. Not yet.
Frazer	And what about Vala, do you think she'd agree?

Blake	We might convince her to go.
Frazer	I think she'd stay.
Blake	What makes you so sure?
Frazer	She has needs met here.
Blake	You mean her drugs?
Frazer	They're prescribed.
Blake	She doesn't really need them.
Frazer	But Dr. Skinner believes she does need them to harmonize her chaotic state.
Blake	But if you helped Sandra get rid of her...
Frazer	I'm sure that's not an immediate concern for Dr. Skinner.
Blake	Why not? He's a doctor isn't he?
Frazer	A research doctor, and you have to keep in mind that Walden's operating expenses depend upon her ovum production, as well as it does on your biological supply.
Blake	But how is getting rid of Vala going to put Walden's financial interest in jeopardy?
Frazer	Dr. Skinner believes that Sandra's problem can be used for the good of the community.
Blake	How so?
Frazer	He's trying to regulate her body's ovulation with their dual personalities, and anything that prevents that opportunity would not be in the interest of Walden.
Blake	Like separating Vala from Sandra.
Frazer	Just between you and I...Exactly.

Blake   Walden, Walden, that's all I hear. His little paradise. What about Sandra's health? Isn't she important too? Isn't that in the interest of Walden?

Frazer   Not immediately.

Blake   Then when will he help her?

Frazer   I don't know. But he has allowed me to continue my research on their problem.

Blake   But you haven't found anything yet.

Frazer   Nothing concrete. But I'll keep my promise. But remember, it's on my own time, not Walden's.

Blake   All right.

Frazer   We should finish Walden's business for now. (He takes out needle) We have a new customer, and Dr. Skinner needs to close the contract today.

Blake   Do we have to do this now?

Frazer   No choice!

Blake   They're still sore from last week.

Frazer   I'll be gentle as possible.

Blake   You always say that.

Frazer   I know, but I mean it.

Blake   Do you know how it feels to go to the bathroom after that thing's been shoved into me?

Frazer   Not really. But we have to do it. Your sperm count contributes to a huge amount of Walden's operating expenses, so I've been told.

Blake   But it hurts every time.

Frazer   I have my orders, Blake, you know that?

Blake   But why me, why not someone else?

Frazer   Your genes are in top shape, and no one else has any like you.

Blake   (Evasive) Why are mine so special?

Frazer   Because of your biological ancestors. You have inherited ideal gene types from them.

Blake   What else do you know about them?

Frazer   I've seen their dossier—that's all.

Blake   Tell me what you know about them?

Frazer   They're exceptionally bright.

Blake   Do you remember their names?

Frazer   No I don't. I don't even know their personal identities, all I know is their numerical values on their dossier.

Blake   Tell me the numbers and I'll get this over with.

Frazer   I'm not sure if I should.

Blake   Come on, they're only a bunch of numbers

Frazer   All right. The female record is marked 3942A, and the male's is 3942B. That's all I know, are you happy now?

Blake   Somewhat.

Frazer.   Good. Now I must have my sample.

Blake   I really don't feel up to this, didn't Dr. Skinner say there was some other way I could give you a sample, it's just that my testicles are still sore.

Frazer   He's considering it, but for now, you'll have to give me a sample this way. (More authoritarian) Assume the position!

Blake   All right. (He drops his pants. Frazer then reveals the needle) Watch it, ah? You'd better not miss.

Frazer   Well don't move then, you know what happens when you move.

Blake   Ahhhh!!! Damn! You missed!!!

Frazer   I said don't move. There, hold still.

Blake   Ouch! Damn it hurts, like always.

Frazer   Just think of all those babies you're going to create.

Blake   Hey, by the way, how many babies would that create?

Frazer   Theoretically, about 500 million, but practically a lot less.

Blake   Why a lot less?

Frazer   Well, before Dr. Skinner hands it over to his clients, he filters out the weaker ones.

Blake   How does he determine that?

Frazer   Colour! Some of your sperm has a jaundice colour, others are too dark in molecular content, and he also destroys those which have too much hemoglobin pigmentation. So, after his selection, he has a lot less to offer to his clients, and that's why you have to provide so much of it. I'm finished—you're free to go.

Blake   (He gets up in pain) Oh it still hurts. You'll ask him for the next one, huh? Won't you?

Frazer   I'll let you know about Dr. Skinner's response as soon as he makes a decision.

Blake   Fine. I'll be with Sandra in the mean time.

Frazer   Tell her I said "hello."

Blake   I will.

He leaves.

Scene 3

Dr. Skinner makes a call. This may be done either by phone or by video-phone technology via the computer.

Skin.   Hello, this is Dr. Skinner at Walden. I am returning the Minister's call. Thank you. Yes. This is Dr. Skinner. Have you had time to read the complete dossier? Oh, Good. Well, I'm very happy that you believe in this project. Yes. I've worked on Blake's dossier for the greater part of my career. If you're going to support it, you have every right to know of course. A personal question? No. I don't mind. Yes, but before I tell you, I must ask for your complete discretion. Thank you. Actually, I am Blake's biological donor. Well, I believe in this project enough to have taken that risk. Yes, sure. Well, my initial intention was to extend his life by removing any chances of sickness. Absolutely, none yet. He has no flaw structurally that would cause that. No, Blake does not know that I'm his biological donor. No one here at Walden does. Yes, a few others in the professional community and of course those who are currently funding the project. Are you still interested in providing support? Thank you. I'm sure you'll be satisfied with your commitment. No, I understand you're very busy. Yes, yes. I will be sending you a sample this week along with a copy of the report. I would appreciate it if you could arrange to forward the first payment after that. Thank you. You too. I'll be in contact with you in a couple of weeks to keep you posted on the progress of the project. Good bye. (Paging Dr. Frazer) Dr. Frazer, could you see me as soon as possible.

> *Dr. Skinner continues to be engaged with the computer until Dr. Frazer arrives.*

Frazer   You called for me, Dr. Skinner?

Skin.   Yes. Have you completed your tests?

Frazer   Yes. I have, Dr. Skinner.

Skin.   What about my suspicions, am I right?

Frazer   You are. The girls' urine test confirms that they are pregnant. Also, the results of the BEST test that I ran on Blake yesterday strongly suggests that he had an unprotected conjugal encounter with one of them.

Skin.   Sandra!

Frazer   Yes. It seems so, but how do we know for certain that Blake actually impregnated Sandra, when in fact it might have been with Vala?

Skin.   That's possible, anyhow, how many weeks do you figure they are?

Frazer   Six weeks.

Skin.   (Going to the intercom) Blake, Sandra, I want to talk to you as soon as possible.

> *Returning to Frazer.*

Frazer   Also, I followed up on her urine test with a test on the embryonic fluid, and the results suggest an abnormality.

Skin.   You mean a genetic defect?

Frazer   I'm not entirely sure yet, but there is some sort of defect, yes.

Skin.   Interesting. Continue with a full analysis, would you. That may prove helpful.

Frazer   As you wish.

Skin. What about Blake's other responses on the BEST test. Are there any other changes happening in him?

Frazer Yes. There are more.

Skin. What are they?

Frazer It seems that Blake's conscience is developing outside the parameters of your program.

Skin. Outside my program—in what way?

Frazer The comparative analysis that I just completed reveals that his responses are different to earlier tests taken.

Skin. How long have the changes been occurring?

Frazer At least three months.

Skin. How do you figure that?

Frazer I've performed a variety of different tests on him since I've arrived, and I noticed that these discrepancies began about that time.

Skin What are the changes this week?

Frazer (Taking his response sheet) To the question, 'do you feel that humans are free to sexually stimulate themselves?,' Blake, for the first time, asked for what purpose. In fact, he categorized possible scenarios this time, as if Walden's justifications were not absolutely credible for him anymore.

Skin So how did you go about affirming Walden's rule?

Frazer I then demanded either a "yes" or a "no," and he responded with a "yes." This is a definite change since our last test. A discrepancy was notable between his verbal response and his inner physiological pattern mapped out on the screen. This time, the response was delayed.

Skin   But did he continue to argue against being sampled?

Frazer Well, today he adamantly refused to give a sample by needle extraction. It's becoming a real pain, for me too, I mean his playful disagreement. But he did seem to be open to a new method, and since we have a change in our response to question number one, perhaps we should make that change now?

Skin.   What type of change were you thinking of?

Frazer Would you mind if we changed to a less painful method?

Skin   No, I don't mind at all, as long as it achieves the same output. The only other method that I can think of is manual extraction, and of course he'd have to perform it himself.

Frazer But...

Skin   But what?

Frazer But Blake might not know how to do that in a such a technical manner?

Skin   Then teach him.

Frazer You mean you want me to teach him how to extract his own sperm?

Skin   For technical purposes, yes. Remember, Mr. Frazer, this is a research center, and we depend on Blake's supply to keep this place operating. You must not think of this with a sexual overtone. It's for scientific purposes.

Frazer All right, I will.

Skin   Good. What about the other changes?

Frazer   To the question, 'Do you accept having multiple partners for the purpose of sexual pleasure?,' he answered "no" instead this time. And even with this change, there was no discrepancy with his inner physiological pattern, because there was no time delay. Something has changed here.

Skin   His conscience!

Frazer   And it's further noticeable on his next response. To the third question, there was also a change, and this time, a delay as well, as if there was a struggle between his inner physiological being and his outer self. It seems that Blake's belief about polygamy has changed, and that a moral element has entered into it.

Skin.   Are you saying that my program is losing its affect on him?

Frazer   Unfortunately, yes.

Skin.   But how?

Frazer   There seems to be another influence on his conscience.

Skin   What other influence?

Frazer   Well, from what I've observed since I have befriended him, I believe it's Sandra.

Skin.   What is she doing to him?

Frazer   She seems to be reprogramming him.

Skin.   No, that can't be. Her influence can't be that much on him, can it?

Frazer   He's been so attached to her these past weeks, even to the dismay of Vala.

Skin   But she doesn't even know what to program him with.

Frazer   I believe you're forgetting her religious influence. In that sense, she has a program to offer him—in fact a highly moral one too—and this would explain the dilemma we are now facing.

Skin   I see. What other changes have you observed happening in him?

Frazer   This one I think you'll be content with. When I asked him about Walden's rule of protected sex, there was no discrepancy. He seems to agree with it still. You look puzzled?

Skin   But why didn't he implement it with his conjugal exchange?

Frazer   Perhaps his response to the following question will help us. When Blake was asked 'Have you had a sexual encounter lately?,' he responded with "yes." But when I followed with the question of Walden's protected sex rule, even he agreed to the importance of the rule, but there was a definite discrepancy. He lied, and this puzzles me.

Skin   Good.

Frazer   That I'm puzzled?

Skin   No. He still feels ethically accountable to Walden's rules.

Frazer   But not another human, why not?

Skin   That's relative.

Frazer   Why?

Skin.   Because his has been educated to behave differently towards them both.

Frazer   Are you saying that he's been trained to be more faithful to Walden than any other human being?

Skin.	Exactly. The human issue should be relative. This means that his conscience still can be changed, with respect to human issues, but not with institutional matters.
Frazer	Because that's absolute?
Skin	Yes. What about his response to terminating the pregnancy?
Frazer	Blake agreed to this principal, and there was no discrepancy.
Skin	Good. What I hoped for.
Frazer	How so?
Skin	First, he should feel morally bad for breaking the unprotected sex rule. But, once I inform him that I know he has disobeyed the rules and that the child is deformed, the termination would be a way of redeeming himself. It's inevitable that he will opt for that choice, since the first factor is absolute—in that he knows he can't raise a child here—it's against Walden's rules.
Frazer	Your plan has an interesting method to it, but I think you've miscalculated one important factor.
Skin	(Somewhat angered) And what is that?
Frazer	Sandra's religious beliefs. I believe she will refuse to terminate the embryo.
Skin.	How are you so certain?
Frazer	Her absolute is, 'Thou Shall Not Kill'.
Skin.	Maybe you're right. But she did give into her compulsion when she slept with him, so she could be persuaded to explain away her belief in abortion on that basis.
Frazer	Persuaded how?

Skin.	That program you've been working on, for that health insurance company, all you'd have to do is explain to her how it functions.
Frazer	And when would I do that?
Skin.	I'll let you know.
Frazer	Fine. But, we don't have any authorization to perform an abortion here—we would have to refer her to a clinic.
Skin.	Not really. We could by administering the RU-486 medication. It's strong enough to terminate the pregnancy within a few days?
Frazer	Yes. But the side effects, the bleeding, the increased heart rate alone, and it hasn't passed final approval yet. I don't think Sandra would agree to any of this.
Skin	(Thinking) If all else fails, we could appeal to Vala instead.
Frazer	But is that ethical?
Skin	Well, certainly it's practical, and it's Vala's body too.
Frazer	Yes, but won't Sandra disagree?
Skin.	I don't know, I'm not in the field of speculations, don't you see that I'm a scientist, not a priest?
Frazer	Yes sir. But, I believe she'll feel betrayed. You should consider the consequences much further, before you act, in all due respect, Dr. Skinner.
Skin	I have Mr. Frazer. It could carry grave consequences for the general population here at Walden, and for the community outside Walden if they decide to keep it. So the embryo must be parted with at all cost. Bring me the RU-486 as soon as you can. I will administer it!

Frazer	Yes, sir, but...
Skin	But what Mr. Frazer?
Frazer	I have to sign for that as well.
Skin	Very well, do so, as soon as possible. Thank you.
Frazer	Yes sir.
Skin	Oh, one last thing before you go. Have you any speculations of why the embryo would be defective?
Frazer	No. Not yet.
Skin	Then, I'll look at it too, if you don't mind?
Frazer	Fine. Here is a copy of the embryos' gene print.

Hands him a disk

Skin.	Could you complete a comparative analysis at the same time, with that of Blake and Sandra's DNA?
Frazer	Yes.
Skin	How long do you think it will take?
Frazer	Once I finish examining Blake's sample and a copy of her last ovum print, I should be able to give you a report later today.
Skin	Very well.

Frazer leaves, then Skinner shortly after.

Scene 4

Sandra is unconscious on the floor when Blake finds her.

Blake Wake up. Wake up. Get up.

Sandra (Viciously) Get your hands off of me. Leave me alone.

Blake Vala?

Sandra No, it's me Sandra.

Blake Come on then, get up.

Sandra Blake, it's you. I'm sorry. What happened?

Blake Vala was drinking again.

Sandra What was she drinking this time?

Blake Wine, mixed with some methadone.

Sandra That's why my stomach's burning. Where did she get it?

Blake She stole it from Skinner's office.

Sandra Oh no!

Blake Here, I'll help you.

Sandra Oh God! (She is a little dizzy) Help me. (He helps her sit up) That's better. Did she fool you again?

Blake No, I could smell the methadone this time.

Sandra She didn't try to touch you?

Blake remains quiet.

Sandra Blake, tell me you didn't?

Blake I had to kiss her.

Sandra But you promised me you wouldn't touch her again.

Blake   But she forced me to.

Sandra   How?

Blake   She knows we slept together and that you're pregnant. She was going to tell Skinner.

Sandra   How does she know?

Blake   She knows you skipped your period again.

Sandra   So you gave into her?

Blake   She promised not to tell if I kissed her. I thought it might buy some time until I talked to you.

Sandra   And do you believe she'll keep her promise?

Blake   I hope so.

Sandra   I know she'll tell Dr. Skinner. I shouldn't have allowed it to happen; it's all my fault.

Blake   Hey, it' not all your fault. It's her fault. If she hadn't spiked my drink at dinner, I wouldn't have ended up in your room.

Sandra   But I should have put my clothes back on.

Blake   Why didn't you?

Sandra   I have my reasons.

Blake   I would like to know them.

Sandra   I feared she might have taken over me again.

Blake   That all?

Sandra   No. I love you Blake and when I saw what she had done, I couldn't take that chance again. If we'd only waited until our wedding night, like we agreed to. Now it's too late.

Blake   No it's not, even if you're pregnant.

Sandra   We don't know for sure if I am.

Blake   But you're two months late.

Sandra   Don't worry, I'll have it soon.

Blake   If you're are, we'd better prepare to leave.

Sandra   Why?

Blake   It's against Walden's rules to raise a child here, so he wouldn't let us have it here.

Sandra   Would you leave me?

Blake   Yes.

Sandra   (embracing him) Thanks. But we'll get married as soon as we get out of here, right?

Blake   But, I haven't proposed yet.

Sandra   (Waiting).

Blake   I thought a lot about it last night. (Taking out paper) And when I woke up after having this dream, I wrote this for you. If you don't mind, I'd like you to read it. (He gives it to her) Here.

Sandra   'To see a World in a Grain of Sand, and a Heaven in a Wild flower. Hold Infinity in the palm of your hand, and Eternity in an hour. Life is full of magic and beauty waiting for our senses to awaken. A life without dreams is like a garden without flowers.'

Blake   I wrote it for our engagement—I don't have a ring.

Sandra   It's enough. It's beautiful.

Blake   And I included 'Heaven' in it too.

Sandra   It's probably the best image of Heaven I've had since I've been here. I appreciate you staying up last night to write this for me. It is very touching.

She returns it to him.

Blake   So, do you want to get married?

Sandra   Of course.

Blake   (Gives her back the poem) It's yours now. You've changed my life so much. Before you arrived, I've never dreamed dreams such as the one I had last night. But when you gave yourself to me that night, something happened in me, and now I dream amazing dreams.

Sandra   I'll keep it then. (She puts it away) Blake, what if I am pregnant, do you really think you could leave Walden, you've been here all your life?

Blake   I'd leave with you now, if you wanted to.

Sandra   Where would we go?

Blake   I don't know, yet.

Sandra   How would we support our family?

Blake   (Jokingly) I can always sell my sperm.

Sandra   I'd rather you keep it for our family instead.

Blake   All right. I've never had a job before, but I'll find one.

Sandra   I'm not sure I'll ever be able to work, unless my problem with Vala is solved.

Blake   But Frazer told me he's trying to find a solution for you—he gave me his word.

Sandra   May be we should stay a while longer; he may help us yet?

Blake   It's just that if you're pregnant, Dr. Skinner won't let you stay that much longer—remember the rule.

Sandra   Yes, and I have a feeling that Vala won't leave that easily. She so dependent on that lithium Dr Skinner gives her.

Blake   Well, let me try to convince her to go with us.

Sandra   How will you do that?

Blake   I'll tell her that I'm leaving, and lead her on to the idea that maybe we can work on a relationship.

Sandra   I don't think you should play with her like that.

Blake   We should at least try.

Sandra   No, keep away from her, I'll find another way.

Blake   Fine.

Sandra   Thanks.

Blake   We should be on our way now.

Sandra   Where to?

Blake   While you were out, Skinner called for us.

Sandra   Why does he want to see us?

Blake   I don't know, but he isn't too happy—at least his voice sounded that way.

Sandra   You don't suppose Vala went and told him already?

Blake   I don't think so; she was out of her mind, and if she did, he probably wouldn't have believed her.

Sandra   If he knows that I am pregnant, I would feel a lot better if you told him that we're going to get married?

Blake   Why, we don't have to.

Sandra   It's just that I don't feel comfortable telling Dr. Skinner that I slept with you, without any intentions of marriage, all right?

Blake	Maybe he doesn't know it was with you?
Sandra	I hope so.
Blake	If he brings it up, I will tell him it was Vala, not you.
Sandra	I am not sure that won't solve much.
Blake	Does that mean you're not too happy about what happened that night?
Sandra	No. It's just that I'd feel a lot better if our intentions of marriage were made clear to him.
Blake	All right. If you'd feel better about it that way, then I'll tell him—let's go.

They leave.

Scene 5

Dr. Skinner is examining the embryo print on his computer screen when Blake and Sandra arrive.

Blake	You called for us.
Skin.	Yes. Please sit down—this will take a while.
Blake	We're not in trouble, are we?
Skin.	Why do you ask that?
Blake	Because you're usually upset with us when you paged us.
Skin.	Well, it seems that your newly found admiration has caused some problems here at Walden.
Blake	You mean because we are in love?
Skin.	If you interpret it that way, I guess so.
Sandra	How has it caused problems?

Skin.	Dr. Frazer has informed me that there has been no ovum from the girls, and we are certain now that Vala is pregnant.
Sandra	You mean me?
Skin.	The both of you I guess.
Blake	I'm a father for real?
Skin.	Not quite yet Blake.
Sandra	But he is.
Skin.	As you wish. But, do you wish to remain pregnant?
Sandra	Yes. I do. Blake has promised to marry me, isn't that right Blake?
Skin.	Is that right, Blake?
Blake	I guess so.
Sandra	Blake. You promised me.
Blake	Yes, I did.
Skin.	But are you sure Blake is the father?
Sandra	Of course I know he is.
Skin.	How are you so sure, Vala might have conceived with someone else.
Sandra	I know because Dr. Frazer was taking ovum from me that same day.
Skin.	When Blake and Vala had a sexual encounter?
Blake	Well, that is not how it exactly happened?
Skin.	But Vala was involved at some point in the affair?
Sandra	You could say that. In fact, if it wasn't for her fooling around with Blake, I would not be pregnant.

Skin.	(Notating Sandra's admission) Then the child is hers?
Sandra	No!
Skin.	Sandra, I find your response very difficult to understand—because of what you've been propagating around here for the last three months.
Sandra	Yes. I know. Please forgive me—but the child is mine.
Skin.	At least half of it is. And you didn't take any means to protect yourselves? You've broken another of Walden's rules.
Blake	Look, we're sorry, but it happened so quickly.
Sandra	Blake is right. It happened so quickly.
Skin.	Then, let's settle this quickly too.
Sandra	I guess you see me as a hypocrite now, don't you Dr. Skinner?
Skin.	I thought I could depend upon your honesty and integrity, but I'm faced with something unpredictable, and I'll have to enforce the rules no matter what you both desire.
Blake	The rules should be changed.
Sandra	Or maybe we should refrain from expressing our love for one another here?
Skin.	I'd be more content with that view.
Sandra	I guess we'll have to go elsewhere, right Blake?
Blake	Yes, maybe that's a good idea.
Skin.	You mean outside of Walden?
Sandra	Yes. Maybe it's better that we leave?

Skin.	But you must keep in mind that the both of you wouldn't have access to the kind of care that is provided for you here—free of charge.
Blake	But Sandra's problem with Vala has not been dealt with as you promised.
Skin.	But Vala's LSD addiction has, and all her medication for this is provided for—free of charge.
Sandra	Her medication has not helped me, and I feel that I'm making no progress.
Skin.	Just because you feel that way, doesn't mean that nothing has been done for your problem.
Sandra	But you promised me over three months ago that if I contributed my ovum to your project, you would try to help me get rid of Vala. You have done nothing, but fill us full of drugs.
Skin.	But you must understand that since you been here, the unpredictable shifts between the two of you have been reduced. These drugs you detest are responsible for this reduction. At least now you can sit and talk with me without the fear of Vala taking over in a matter of seconds, then leaving a few seconds later. I think we've made progress.
Sandra	But will I ever be rid of her one day?
Skin.	I can't commit to that at the moment.
Blake	Or is it because you don't want to get rid of her, for financial reasons maybe?
Skin.	What are you insinuating?
Blake	If you resolved Sandra's disorder, wouldn't that threaten your plan to increase their ovum contribution?

Skin.	That plan is of no interest to me at the moment; she is pregnant, and you can't have it here. You'll have to either part with it or Sandra will have to leave.
Sandra	What do you mean by 'part with it'?
Skin.	Terminate it!
Sandra	I'm not going to kill my child.
Skin.	You mean embryo.
Sandra	I mean—child!
Skin.	But I don't think you have taken into account something very hidden from you at the moment.
Blake	Like what?
Skin.	The embryo is genetically malformed.
Blake	You're lying to us so will go along with your plan.
Sandra	My baby?
Skin.	Yes, unfortunately.
Blake	You're just saying that to keep us here, aren't you?
Skin	(Turning to the computer screen) Dr. Frazer gave me a gene print of the embryo earlier; here it is on the screen. I've examined it myself, and I agree with his diagnosis. You may want to consult with him to confirm it, if you like. But let me assure you, his diagnosis is legitimate.
Blake	I will talk to him.
Sandra	I knew I should have stuck to God's plan.
Blake	You're not thinking that God is angry at you for breaking our vow?
Sandra	(Silent).
Skin.	I guess your God is a cruel God after all?

Sandra   Or maybe this can help me become stronger?

Blake   It doesn't matter whether we were married or not, this would have happened anyway, Sandra. Don't blame yourself. (She doesn't listen to him, then he turns to Skinner) What should we do then?

Skin.   I've asked Dr. Frazer to prepare a medication that will terminate the pregnancy; it's quite normal and harmless too.

Sandra   I refuse to take anymore medication from you.

Skin.   But an abortion by aspirator later will be much more painful.

Sandra   I will not kill our child—don't you see—it's wrong!

Skin.   It's not wrong, it's only normal.

Sandra   God says that we are made in his image, and it is only logical that if I destroy our child, I will be responsible for destroying the humanity of God in me. I will not allow you to take that from me.

Skin.   Blake, do you feel that it's wrong for her to take some medication to remove a defective embryo from her body?

Blake   (Turning to Sandra) Sandra, if it's deformed, we could terminate it—get married then try to have a better one?

Sandra   Blake, don't you see the more important issue?

Blake   No. I don't; it's a medical issue.

Sandra   Just because the baby's not a perfect human being, doesn't give us the right to destroy a human life, it's not natural.

Skin.   But it's deformed, and that is unnatural.

Blake   He's right Sandra—it's unnatural.

Skin.	And a natural solution is a medical solution at this moment.
Sandra	(To Blake) And what if it were found out that you were genetically deformed, does that also give us the right to end your life?
Blake	But I am not an embryo.
Skin.	So, you don't agree with her choice Blake?
Blake	I'm not sure...
Sandra	I want to talk to Dr. Frazer before we go any further.
Skin.	You don't believe me?
Sandra	I have a right to know more—that's all.
Skin.	Very well. I'll notify him that you would like to talk with him.
Sandra	Fine. Blake, remember, you promised me.
Blake	Yes. I remember. I promise.

She leaves. He engages his video screen.

Skin.	Mr. Frazer. Sandra would like to meet with you. Would you prepare that program for her—yes, the one we discussed earlier—yes that's it. Fine. Thank you. (Turing to Blake) Do you think Vala would leave?
Blake	I don't think so.
Skin.	Then, why don't we solve this problem quickly by terminating the pregnancy?
Blake	You know she won't have it.
Skin.	Why are you acting like this?
Blake	Because I want to love her.

Skin.	She's an abnormal person. You're not. God! You were created with hybrid genes. Your DNA history is astronomically better than hers. I can't even understand why you are attracted to her. It's not rational.
Blake	I know it happened so quickly...
Skin.	Then end it quickly!
Blake	I can't!
Skin.	If you get rid of it, you could continue with her here.
Blake	(Wavering) I... she won't have it any other way.
Skin.	But Vala will.
Blake	You'd better not use Vala against us.
Skin.	It's Vala's body too, and her choice as well.
Blake	You're playing her against our lives—it's a game for you, isn't it?
Skin.	But, you must stay here, (Indiscreetly) 'son', you have no other choice—it's for your own good.
Blake	What did you say?
Skin.	I said you have no other choice.
Blake	Oh.
Skin.	Haven't you considered the consequences of your choice? The financial burden alone would crush you out there.
Blake	We'd make it anyway.
Skin.	What insurance company would cover a deformed child. Once they find out, they'll reject your claim. It's a question of thousands of dollars in medical expenses.

Blake	We'll find someone to help us.
Skin.	The only help they'll offer you is the choice I'm offering you now.
Blake	Stop it!
Skin.	Can you imagine living with a deformed child—in pain perhaps because of the deformity—think about that?
Blake	I told you to stop.
Skin.	Where would you get the money for your child's medical expenses?
Blake	I'm not sure at the moment.
Skin.	Then take my offer—now!
Blake	But Sandra wants...
Skin.	But you must try to convince Sandra to go along with it, at least to save the child from suffering.
Blake	Suffering...
Skin.	Yes.
Blake	If I did, would you let us stay here as a married couple?
Skin.	Yes, and you could share a room, but you must follow Walden's contraceptive rules, for the sake of Walden's mandate.
Blake	You promise we could have our own space?
Skin.	Yes.
Blake	I'll talk to her.
Skin.	Good. I knew you would eventually understand. I am very happy with your decision.
Blake	Is that all or can I leave?

Skin.   Oh, before you leave, I talked it over with Frazer, and we decided that we can stop the needle extraction, for your own benefit. He'll help you with the new method, and I can reassure you that there will be no pain involved. We have a new client, and the contract must be settled today.

Blake   All right.

Skin.   Remember, Blake, it comes down to money. It really does.

Scene 6

> *Frazer is examining a DNA print on the computer screen when Sandra arrives.*

Sandra   (Looking over his shoulder) What are you doing?

Frazer   A DNA evaluation for an insurance company.

Sandra   You do a lot of that here?

Frazer   Often enough.

Sandra   I really don't understand science or medicine that well. Would you mind explaining more of it to me?

Frazer   No I don't mind. I have to determine whether it is a healthy DNA strand or not.

Sandra   Okay. But, how do you know the difference between a good one and a bad one?

Frazer   You see this vertical line here that divides the screen?

Sandra   Yes.

Frazer   On the left side is the DNA print of a potential client. I have to compare it to this healthy one on the right, to see if there is a defect. It's like a computer trying to match finger prints.

Sandra   And what happens if you find a defect?

Frazer   I'll send my observations to the company, then they'll decide whether they'll want to insure the applicant.

Sandra   If you find a defect in their applicant's DNA, will they insure their applicant?

Frazer   If the defect causes a higher the normal risk for the company, probably not.

Sandra   I see (Standing in a moment of contemplation).

Frazer   Have I lost you?

Sandra   No. I understand more now. That DNA print on the right side, is it supposed to be a perfect one?

Frazer   Yes, well as perfect as you can get it. But it is a healthy one.

Sandra   Do you know that person well?

Frazer   That's confidential.

Sandra   It's probably Dr. Skinner's?

Frazer   Unofficially, you're probably right. But I can't tell you that for certain.

Sandra   All right. I have another question, if you don't mind?

Frazer   Sure, go ahead.

Sandra   This healthy gene; the one here on the right.

Frazer   Yes, what about it?

Sandra   What if it really wasn't healthy at all, wouldn't your diagnosis be incorrect?

Frazer   If the gene on the right wasn't healthy—yes of course—but the possibility of that happening is highly unlikely.

Sandra   Why?

Frazer   Because I've tested it more than once. In fact, I've tested it many times and I've arrived at the same results; it is a healthy one.

Sandra   But to what gene did you compare it to?

Frazer   I didn't compare it to any gene.

Sandra   Then what did you compare it to?

Frazer   To my knowledge of what a healthy gene is.

Sandra   It's an interesting system you have here.

Frazer   (Very proud) Thanks. It has taken me years of research to develop it.

Sandra   Is this how you discovered my child's deformity?

Frazer   (Change in mood) Yes. Unfortunately.

Sandra   But what led you to check for it?

Frazer   When your body didn't produce any ovum from your last sample, I decided to do a further analysis of your body fluids.

Sandra   I don't remember you doing that.

Frazer   Because I took the sample from Vala.

Sandra   That's why my stomach is sore.

Frazer   Yes, because of the needle. I retrieved a sample of embryonic fluid with it, and from its fluid I took a gene sample, then compared it to this one here on the right.

Sandra   So the gene sample from embryo didn't do well against this one here on your screen?

Frazer	No, it did not.
Sandra	Then no insurance company would help with my child's medical fees?
Frazer	If they diagnose your child using a system like this, probably not. I'm sorry. It's my job to inform you.
Sandra	It's my fault—not yours.
Frazer	Why do you feel that way?
Sandra	I made a promise before God that I wouldn't sleep with Blake until after our wedding, and now this has happened.
Frazer	I don't get it. How would your broken promise change this?
Sandra	Before I slept with Blake, I wanted to do it very much, but God was warning me not to do it. I should have listened.
Frazer	How do you know that for sure?
Sandra	It was like a voice inside of me was saying 'no.' But I gave in, and now this has happened.
Frazer	Now wait a minute, God didn't do this to you at all, and don't blame yourself. Whether you slept with Blake two months ago or two years after your marriage, the mutation might have happened anyway. A gene mutation caused the deformity, not a broken promise.
Sandra	Then why didn't this mutation happen earlier in my or Vala's life?
Frazer	I don't know exactly, yet, but once I finish this gene analysis, I will continue to work on both your DNA prints. I'll do my best to help you find a solution.

Sandra   Do you think you can help my child?

Frazer   I'm not sure yet, but it has been done before with genetic engineering.

Sandra   What's genetic engineering?

Frazer   With the technology we have today, we can manipulate a gene to change its formation—in a way—we can heal it!

Sandra   You can do that here?

Frazer   No, not me. My area is mainly gene diagnosis. But Dr. Skinner's field is genetic engineering.

Sandra   So it might work on my baby?

Frazer   I can't say for sure, but there is a possibility that it could restore the gene back to its natural state.

Sandra   Has it been done successfully before?

Frazer   Absolutely.

Sandra   But can you promise that it would absolutely help my child?

Frazer   No, there is always a risk for the child.

Sandra   Then I'll have my child naturally, just the way he or she is now.

Frazer   That might be a lot of extra suffering—I hope you understand that.

Sandra   I understand! This is my fault and I have to learn to live with the consequences of what I've done— no matter what they are.

Frazer   I don't understand now. We don't even know where the defect originated from yet; it could have been inherited from your parents, or even from Blake's side. Don't blame yourself for this.

Sandra   But I slept with Blake and my baby is a result of that. It's my fault.

Frazer   But it may be a hereditary problem.

Sandra   Let's say you did discover that, how would that change things? Should I blame them, and if so, how is that going to change things? It won't change anything, other than how I feel towards them, and even that won't be for the good probably. I have to live with what I've done, whether it is hereditary or not. You look really puzzled!

Frazer   That's because I've never thought of looking at life that way before.

Sandra   Well, try something new for a change.

She goes to leave.

Frazer   Wait, if I've offended you because of your religious beliefs, I didn't mean to.

Sandra   It's okay, I didn't feel offended. And by the way, thanks for trying to help me.

Frazer   I won't give up, I'll try to find something to help you and your child. I promise.

Sandra   Thank you. I appreciate it very much.

Frazer   You're welcome. But I hope you won't believe that God has done this to you; this is a human error, probably hereditary, don't forget that, all right?

Sandra   All right, Mr. Frazer. I'll try.

She leaves.

END OF ACT ONE

ACT TWO

Scene 1

> *Dr. Skinner arrives as Frazer is working at his computer.*

Skin.   Did you have a chance to present our program to Sandra?

Frazer   Yes. She left a moment ago.

Skin.   Do you think she's conscious of the financial burden ahead of her?

Frazer   Yes. I think so.

Skin.   Good. I'll make a note of this for your final intern evaluation.

Frazer   (Coldly) Thank you.

Skin.   (Looking at the computer screen) Have you finished your diagnosis of their DNA?

Frazer   Yes, and I did find something very interesting about Blake's DNA that you should consider.

Skin.   And what is that?

Frazer   A mutation in Blake's gene.

Skin.   (Looking at the screen) Impossible!

Frazer   Theoretically perhaps, but here it is. (Looking into the computer screen) You can double check it for yourself. The mutation seems to have started here (Then points to screen) I believe it's an alien gene. The DNA fundamentals are not similar to that of Blake's. I've run a comparative analysis of the mutant's molecular structure to that of Blake's, and their structures are completely different.

Skin.   Is this Blake's on the right?

Frazer Yes. Look at the lower left quadrant, the lining colour is different from the one on the right.

Skin.   (Pointing) Here?

Frazer That's it.

Skin.   Do you have any preliminary ideas for the cause of this mutation?

Frazer (Looking directly at Skinner) The gene lining seems to be where it started. The mutation could be an effect of the faulty lining.

Skin.   What do you mean by 'seems to be' —you're not sure?

Frazer I'm having difficulties enhancing the lining further. Every time I attempt to enlarge it, I either sacrifice the quality of the image or the system crashes on me.

Skin.   You can stop then. I'll try it myself.

Frazer Fine. (Gives him a disk) Here, I have a copy for you.

Skin.   Thanks, you needn't work on it any further. I'll take care of it now.

Frazer Someone must have redirected his gene formation earlier in his development?

Skin.   Perhaps, but why have we not found the mutation until now?

Frazer It could be that our technology is much more advance now?

Skin.   Yes, that may be so, but he did undergo extensive monitoring which should have picked it up.

Frazer But since I've been here he hasn't.

Skin. That's because we stopped monitoring him on a regular basis five years ago.

Frazer Why didn't you continue to monitor him?

Skin. We did, but not regularly.

Frazer Why not?

Skin. We had no indicators that anything unnatural was manifesting, so I decided to stop the regular monitoring entirely.

Frazer Didn't you think it was ethical to stop monitor him?

Skin. Yes, there was no reason to continue.

Frazer But what about human error, isn't that reason enough?

Skin. (Angrily) We had no signs of anything occurring.

Frazer Okay, I'm not trying to blame you. I'm just trying to find an answer—that's all.

Skin. But why the mutation now, and not years ago?

Frazer It could have been agitated after Blake and Sandra exchanged body fluids.

Skin. Or perhaps her body perpetrated the mutation?

Frazer I don't believe so.

Skin. Why, what did you find with her analysis?

Frazer There is no sign of any mutation. Paradoxically, she's genetically perfect.

Skin. Did you make a copy of her gene print on this disk as well?

Frazer Yes, it's there with Blake's.

Skin. I'll double check it.

Frazer	Fine. How long have you been selling his sperm?
Skin.	About four years.
Frazer	How many samples have you retrieved from him?
Skin.	About two hundred.
Frazer	To how many clients did you sell them to?
Skin.	Hundreds.
Frazer	To couples mostly?
Skin.	No, other clinics as well.
Frazer	Do you have their records up to date?
Skin.	Of course I do, some are still our clients.
Frazer	Then you must notify them as soon as possible.
Skin.	I will certainly not notify them at the present.
Frazer	At least the clinics should be notified so they can begin their own independent diagnosis.
Skin.	Now, wait a minute. We must take some precautions before acting in that manner.
Frazer	What sort of precautions?
Skin.	I want to know exactly how the gene mutated first—before I include anyone else in this. Is that clear, Mr. Frazer?
Frazer	As you wish. But please keep in mind the consequences of prolonging that.
Skin.	Such as?
Frazer	Blake and Sandra's desire to leave Walden. If they leave, you'll have no control on what is found later or how it is interpreted.
Skin.	But how are you so sure they'll leave?

Frazer   Sandra has made a decision to raise her child, no matter what the consequences will be.

Skin.   That may be her desire, but not Vala's. She has already informed me that she is more than willing to part with it. That is why I requested that you prepare the RU-486 medication. Is it ready?

Frazer   Yes (He takes out the package but is hesitant to give it to him) but...

Skin.   Good. I'll administer it for you.

Frazer   But what about Sandra's...

Skin.   (Forcefully) Sandra will have to make a sacrifice for the sake of the community.

Frazer   I'm not sure whether this is a good solution to Walden's immediate problems.

Skin.   If Sandra leaves with it, it could create a genetic nightmare for all of us, even the community out there would not want to suffer those consequences?

Frazer   No. I don't think so. But have you considered any other options?

Skin.   Like what?

Frazer   Gene therapy. You could perform it on the embryo. You might heal her baby.

Skin.   Well, yes, but I would have no ovum from her either. No, our immediate problem is more important. Give it to me.

Frazer   All right (He gives it to him) She must take this one first, then if it hasn't evacuated by the following day, the second must be taken. She should be monitored very closely after taking the second one because her heart rate will increase considerably. On the third day, her body will empty it out.

Skin.   Very well, we will.

Frazer   But we haven't solved our problem completely. What if Sandra decides to leave anyway, and Blake with her. What are you going to do about Blake?

Skin.   What are the extreme consequences of his mutation?

Frazer   Well, if you examine the synthetic lining, you'll find that it's severed. Once it begins to disintegrate, his cortisone will eventually overflow like a fountain into his blood stream. He will have unpredictable outbreaks of energy—or anger.

Skin.   You mean violence, don't you?

Frazer   Possibly, if the disintegration of the lining has a domino effect.

Skin.   He could even attack a person without any restraint to what he's doing?

Frazer   Possibly.

Skin.   And he probably won't be able to control it?

Frazer. If we don't find a solution.

Skin.   So, if he leaves and this happens, he might end up killing someone?

Frazer   It's purely speculative at this moment.

Skin.   Even Sandra or his child?

Frazer   (More assured this time) I said it's purely speculative.

Skin.   Or someone from the community.

Frazer   We can't say that for certain.

Skin.	But highly possible though?
Frazer	Unfortunately yes. What are you contemplating?
Skin.	If our plan with Vala fails, we'll need to prepare a D.A.S program for him, immediately.
Frazer	Wait a minute! This is ludicrous!
Skin.	But, there is still hope that once Vala terminates the pregnancy, they will stay. But if not, then we'll plan for a D.A.S. as soon as possible. So you should prepare the drug for him, we can always abort it, if he decides to stay...Are you listening to me?
Frazer	I hear you...But is this right?
Skin.	If we have his consent. But we should begin a dossier as soon as possible though.
Frazer	What about a third party?
Skin.	We don't have much time to work that out.
Frazer	But we need another doctor's opinion.
Skin.	You'll be that second opinion. As long as you sign the dossier, along with my accreditation, we'll be okay.
Frazer	I'd rather not sign for his death.
Skin.	(Forcing him) Damn! What if Blake leaves Walden. He'll be a genetic land mine out there. We can't allow that to happen, if we did...God! Just prepare it, just in case, but he must not leave!
Frazer	All right, I'll do it.
Skin.	Very well. But let me explain it to him. I'll take care of that part. You just sign for the medication.
Frazer	Fine.

He leaves.

Scene 2

Sandra is sitting alone when Blake arrives.

Blake   Sandra?

Sandra Yes, it's me Blake. (He touches her, but she evades him) Please stop. We shouldn't behave like this now.

Blake   It's you all right.

Sandra Have you talked to Dr. Frazer yet?

Blake   Yes—a moment ago.

Sandra Did you ask him about our test results?

Blake   Yes, but he said we have to talk to Dr. Skinner about them.

Sandra It's my fault—the baby and all.

Blake   Oh come on—it's not all that bad.

Sandra Isn't it?

Blake   But it's not the end of the world. We can still be together—think about that instead.

Sandra You really don't feel bad about it—do you?

Blake   Not really, well...It's just that Skinner knows that we didn't protect ourselves. If we had, he wouldn't be so angry.

Sandra But we will have the baby.

Blake   If we have it, then we'll have to leave.

Sandra (Getting up to leave) Then we'll leave.

Blake   (Stopping her) I am not convinced that we should do that right now.

Sandra Why not?

Blake   I think you should consider what it's...sorry, the baby's going to cost us if we leave here.

Sandra   Ah, so that's what Dr. Skinner filled your mind with when I left. Don't listen to him—trust me instead.

Blake   I think you're being a little bit too idealistic.

Sandra   And I think you're being a bit too much like a tape recorded robot.

Blake   Can we keep our conversation on a rational level, please?

Sandra   Does that mean I should reserve myself from being emotional?

Blake   If you want to be more human about this, I think so.

Sandra   I'll think about it, but what else did he plant in your mind?

Blake   He said no insurance company would pay for the medical expenses, once they discovered the genetic problems.

Sandra   Unfortunately, insurance companies only want to insure healthy people.

Blake   Are you being sarcastic against me or the insurance companies?

Sandra   (Jokingly) What do think is more irrational?

Blake   You still love me, don't you?

Sandra   Yes. Of course I do.

Blake   Then, why don't we get married and stay here.

Sandra   How are we going to do that?

Blake   Dr Skinner told me we could live here together.

Sandra	He did?
Blake	Yes. On the conditions that we follow his contraceptive rule and...no children.
Sandra	But what about our baby?
Blake	We'd have to dispose of it.
Sandra	'Dispose of it.' Why don't you just wrap it up in a glad bag and throw it away then. Our child is a human being, and I can't allow that—it's wrong.
Blake	Please calm down.
Sandra	'Dispose of it.'
Blake	All right, I'm sorry, but Sandra, it's not even born.
Sandra	That doesn't convince me either.
Blake	But how can you accept it as a human at this point?
Sandra	Do you think that a dog will come out of here, or better yet a monkey?
Blake	Don't be absurd!
Sandra	I'm not joking; this is our child; she or he will come out of me, look like me perhaps, probably act like me, or maybe like you—that's a fact and that's natural!
Blake	But a malformed embryo is not natural.
Sandra	(Crying) Do you think I want my baby to be that way?
Blake	(He holds her) No, I'm sorry, I didn't mean to hurt you.
Sandra	So, that's what he talked to you about after I left.
Blake	Yes.

Sandra   What else did he tell you?

Blake   We talked about how the mutation occurred.

Sandra   How does he know, when I talked to Frazer, he told me that the analysis wasn't completed yet, that's why I came looking for him now. But what did he say?

Blake   He said the mutation occurred because of your psychotic state.

Sandra   Oh, he did, and you believe him?

Blake   I'm not sure. Maybe he's right.

Sandra   Dr. Frazer also told me that because Dr. Skinner is a genetic engineer he could perform some type of genetic engineering on our child, which might heal our baby.

Blake   Well, Dr. Skinner's field is genetic engineering, but whether he wants to help us with that is another thing.

Sandra   We should at least see him about that option. You could help me convince him—you have known him longer than I have. It might work.

Blake   But what if it does not? Would you still want to keep it?

Sandra   Yes.

Blake   Why?

Sandra   Because our child is what connects us. Forever! Before this child came along, you didn't have a family and neither did I. Now we do. Don't you see how this child brings us together? Blake?

Blake   But will it bring us closer together?

Sandra   Yes. I'll know you as a father, and you'll know me as a mother. I know it will be a sacrifice Blake. But this is what will bring us closer.

Blake   But what about other sacrifices—for us?

Sandra   I won't kill our child!

Blake   But it's deformed, and if we let it live, it will suffer so much because we allowed it to.

Sandra   And I guess suffering's a bad thing for you too?

Blake   Of course it is. No one wants to suffer, not anybody in their right mind.

Sandra   But don't you think suffering is necessary for us to grow closer together too?

Blake   A screwed up child and now suffering too, is there anything nice going to bring us closer?

Sandra   Maybe—love.

Pause between them.

Blake   There's just one thing that bothers me.

Sandra   And what's that?

Blake   Vala. Skinner told me she is against having the child, or for that matter leaving here.

Sandra   I will not let her kill our child.

Blake   But Vala is easily manipulated by Dr Skinner.

Sandra   But if we get her to leave, she won't be, you have to try.

Blake   You mean you want me now to get her to help us?

Sandra   Yes, she wants you so bad, and she'll just about do anything to get you. Let's use that to our advantage.

Blake   But your plan may get me into trouble again.

Sandra	Sooner or later, I'll have to live with the idea of her you together, but for now, you'll have to get her to do what we want.
Blake	All right.
Sandra	Good. Let's go convince Dr. Skinner now.

Scene 3

> *Dr. Skinner is sitting at his computer examining Blake's DNA print that Frazer has given him when Blake and Sandra arrive.*

Skin.	(Alone) Damn! It can't be! Why now?
Sandra	Are we interrupting?
Skin.	No. I was thinking out loud—that's all.
Sandra	Dr. Frazer mentioned that we should see you about our test results.
Skin.	Yes, that's right. Please, sit here (By the computer) I have the results here on the screen.
Sandra	So, you know exactly why the child is deformed?
Skin.	(Hesitant) Yes.
Blake	Well?
Skin.	Mr. Frazer has found that your embryo's mutation has been inherited from Blake.
Blake	It's my fault?
Skin.	Unfortunately, yes. It was a surprise to me too.
Sandra	Dr. Frazer discovered this?
Skin.	(Pointing to the screen) Yes, he gave me this gene print to examine it myself, and I agree with his diagnosis.

Blake   But you've always told me…

Skin.   I know. But you have the truth before you now.

Sandra   I want an explanation, please.

Skin.   (Pointing to the computer screen) Dr. Frazer has found that this lining here in Blake's DNA has mutated. If you look at Blake's print on the right side here, you'll see that there is a parallel characteristic, with that of the embryos' lining here. They're identical in malformation. Blake passed it on by your conjugal act; the unprotected one we discussed earlier.

Blake   What can we do?

Skin.   Nothing. It's too late.

Sandra   What about genetic engineering? Isn't that your expertise?

Skin.   Yes, it is.

Sandra   Could you heal our baby, then?

Skin.   No. I can't reverse this process back to its natural state, because...

Sandra   Because what?

Skin.   Because there are unnatural stages at work now, and I am no longer able to reverse them.

Blake   What will happen to me then?

Skin   Dr. Frazer informed me—if the lining continues to degrade—there will be an increased flow of cortisone into your blood stream.

Sandra   And what does that mean for us?

Skin.   An extreme level of cortisone flow into his brain cells will violently affect his whole being.

Blake   In what way?

Skin.	Extreme amounts of energy, swelling body parts, and an increase in your blood pressure when your heart rate increases. Essentially, this will lead to violent manifestations.
Blake	I am going to be violent.
Skin.	Yes, which means you could harm Sandra or your child?
Sandra	But there must be something you can do to help?
Skin.	Well, if we could foresee a violent reaction about to occur, heavy sedation would prevent him for hurting anyone. But have you noticed any abnormal or rapid physiological changes recently?
Blake	These red scars on my arm.
Skin.	Let me see it, please. (Blake shows him) How long has it been there?
Blake	Just this week; they were very small at first, then by this morning, they became bumpy.
Skin.	It's changing faster than I thought.
Sandra	How can we prevent him from becoming violent?
Skin.	I do have a short term solution with medication.
Sandra	Could he function properly on this medication?
Skin.	It depends upon the level of dosage, he could lose half the feeling or even more of his motor skills.
Sandra	You mean, he'd feel like he was stoned all the time?
Skin.	Well, if his dosage was high enough, he would lose some consciousness.
Sandra	I'd rather you not be drugged up at all Blake.
Skin.	But that's asking him to suffer a great amount of pain.

Blake   Is there another option?

Skin.   Yes and no suffering. And no drugs on a regular basis.

Blake   What is that?

Skin.   I believe…that Blake should undergo a D.A.S. program for the sake of the community.

Sandra   What is a D.A.S.?

Skin.   A project termination program. Dr. Frazer has agreed to assist; it is for your well being and for the protection of everyone around you.

Sandra   (Angry at Dr. Skinner) What do you mean by a 'termination program'?

Skin.   Doctor assisted suicide.

Blake   Do you mean you'd want to do this now?

Skin.   As soon as possible.

Sandra   (Standing up) This is enough!

Skin.   He won't live much longer anyway, nor even be able to fulfill his duties as a husband or father, for that matter.

Sandra   You can't just shut a human being off because it doesn't work properly. He's a human! You must help him instead.

Skin.   I don't think we can help him, that's my problem. And in light of what Dr. Frazer has diagnosed, Blake's problem must be dealt with before he hurts anyone—including you or your child.

Sandra   (Getting angrier) Blake we're leaving now!

Skin.   Blake, I've helped you all your life. I've almost been like a father to you, I'll try my best, but as for your suffering…

Sandra   We don't need your help anymore! We'll get help elsewhere.

Skin.   And where would you go? His problem would cost you thousands of dollars. Who would be willing to give you that amount of help?

Sandra   There must be a doctor out there who will help us?

Skin.   Perhaps, but once an insurance company receives Blake's preliminary analysis, and of your baby's, you won't be able to afford their help.

Blake   Sandra. He's right.

Sandra   (Angry at Blake) No he's not!

Skin.   So it would be better for you both, if I remained here at Walden.

Sandra   Blake, he'll destroy you, don't you understand that! (She loses her patience and screams, and at this point Vala takes over Sandra) Fuck right off! Don't fuck with my mind. What are you fucking doing to me?

Skin.   Vala? Everything's fine. Calm down. Please sit down. I was just informing Blake and Sandra about the embryos' genetic problems that were inherited from Blake.

Vala   Blake? But you told us that was impossible.

Skin.   We thought so too, but things have changed.

Vala   It's your damn fault?

Blake   I guess, so you can stop blaming Sandra.

Skin.   Please, stop, the both of you. This is dead serious. (Turning to Vala) You don't want a deformed child, do you Vala?

Vala   No, for fuck sakes.

Skin.	Then you do want to end the pregnancy?
Vala	(Looking for Blake's reaction) Yes.
Blake	(Looking at Skinner) You'd better not use her against Sandra. That would kill her.
Vala	Than I would be all by myself.
Blake	And what about being with me?
Vala	Why should I do something for you?
Blake	This child will bring us closer together.
Skin.	But if you did that for him, you would have to leave here, and give up your treatment—all the benefits of living here would end too.
Vala	All right. It's screwed up anyway, Blake.
Blake	But Sandra wants...
Vala	It's my body too, and I really don't give a fuck what she wants.
Blake	But I want to be the father.
Skin.	You wouldn't be a father for that long, anyhow, Please keep that in mind too.
Vala	But I don't want to give birth to a fucked up child.
Blake	Is that because you don't want to be around a fucked up person—like you?
Vala	Fuck you both!
Skin.	Please stop it Vala, that's enough. The both of you must stop fighting now. Blake, please leave us alone. I want to discuss this with Vala, without anymore arguing.
Blake	But...
Skin.	But nothing—leave now.

Blake   (Getting up to leave) You'd better not, that's all I've got to say.

           He leaves.

Skin.   I am glad he didn't win you over. This is absurd.

Vala   I'm sure he doesn't care two-shits about me anymore.

Skin.   So, what are we waiting for?

Vala   All right, I'll end it. What do you want me to do?

Skin.   (Taking out the RU-486) If you take this, the pregnancy will terminate within three days.

Vala   Give it to me then. (Taking the package) How do I take it?

Skin   When you take it, you'll need to wear a sanitary napkin until it's flushed out from your body. It will appear, somewhat like your menstruation period, but it won't last as long, and don't worry, it is a harmless drug, and you'll have no pain.

Vala   How much do I take?

Skin.   You'll take it in two parts (He gives her a cup of water) You may take the first installment now if you'd like?

Vala   I'd rather have a sanitary napkin on before I take it, if you don't mind?

Skin.   No, that'll be fine. I'll ask Dr. Frazer to check up on you later. If you feel a little drowsy after taking it, please rest. Don't forget, Sandra will try to stop you, so it's important that you do this as soon as possible.

Vala   Fine (She goes to leave then stops) You said no pain, ah?

Skin.   Absolutely none.

Vala	Good.

She leaves and shortly after Dr. Frazer arrives. Dr. Skinner is still sitting at his computer, examining the screen.

Frazer	Have you had time to examine Blake's DNA print?
Skin.	No, I'm not finished yet. Did you prepare the drug for Blake?
Frazer	Yes, as you ordered.
Skin.	Did you bring it?
Frazer	No. You said we should wait to see whether Vala will take the RU-486 first. Did you give it to her?
Skin.	Yes, and you should begin to monitor her.
Frazer	I will (He goes to leave).
Skin.	Wait a minute. Bring me the drug for Blake instead.
Frazer	But you said...
Skin.	I know what I said, but the situation has changed and we need to act as quickly as possible; they may leave!
Frazer	I don't believe you're rational.
Skin.	But we have no choice! If Blake leaves here in his condition, the community will suffer. I can't allow that, Mr. Frazer. He could harm someone drastically, don't you understand that?
Frazer	Very well.

He leaves then Dr. Skinner.

Scene 4

Vala is alone holding the RU-486 when Dr. Frazer crosses her path.

Frazer   Do you know what that will do?

Vala   For Christ sakes—of course I do.

Frazer   Oh, I'm sorry, I thought you were Sandra.

Vala   (Harshly) Sorry if I disappointed you.

Frazer   So, have you taken any of it yet?

Vala   No—not yet.

Frazer   Have you decided yet?

Vala   Who the hell do you think you are?

Frazer   I'm just doing my job.

Vala   Then do your job.

Frazer   Do you want to have the child?

Vala   I couldn't care less about it.

Frazer   Blake does.

Vala   No. He only gives a shit about it because she wants it.

Frazer   But maybe it's because he loves her and wants to respect her choice?

Vala   Blake doesn't love her. He's only sticking around her because he knocked her up.

Frazer   How are you so sure?

Vala   Do you believe she peeled off her clothes for him?

Frazer   It does seem a bit odd for her.

Vala   That's because she didn't.

Frazer   I don't get it?

Vala	It was me. I spiked his milk at supper that night with some methadone. And when I got him into my room, I got off his clothes.
Frazer	But Blake told to me he slept with Sandra—not you.
Vala	That's right, too bad for me. Just I was about to screw his brains out, the bitch moved in for the kill. The last thing I remember was looking at his body, there on the bed and thinking how beautiful it was. Then...I know you are going to think I am lying, but I was afraid to.
Frazer	It does seem odd for you.
Vala	Thanks, but I'm not lying. I had this different feeling. I wasn't sure, that's all. It was fun enough being there with him, but I lost my chance.
Frazer	So you knew all along that Blake and Sandra were together?
Vala	Not really. I asked him later but he denied it. He told me she got dressed and told him to leave. Knowing her, I believed him, until she missed her period, so I asked him again, but he lied to me. Then when she didn't bleed this week, I knew that the little bitch did screw him. What a little slut ah? She walks around telling everyone how good she is, then behind closed doors her sinful nature is allowed to bear fruit. Well that fucking fruit is soar!
Frazer	You sound a bit soar—is that why you want to go ahead with the abortion?
Vala	It's my body too, and I can get rid of a screwed up child if I want to.
Frazer	But even you said it was her who slept with him, not you.

Vala	It's my body too! And I'm not going to give her a chance to get between us.
Frazer	How do you think Blake will feel about you once you've aborted his child?
Vala	He's a big boy.
Frazer	He might even hate you?
Vala	You don't know that for sure.
Frazer	And this might be an opportunity to gain his respect.
Vala	He does loves her more than me...
Frazer	How do you know that, you're never present when they're together?
Vala	I can feel what she feels when he's around.
Frazer	You can sense her emotions, even when you can't see or hear what is happening to her?
Vala	Yes. It all started after she slept with him. It all makes sense now. I feel those feelings she is having with him when they're together.
Frazer	Then if you knew they did, why did you persist in pushing him to confess it?
Vala	Because until now I've never put the two together. But now I know. I feel her feelings when they are together. I want him to feel that way for me!
Frazer	But he only loves her.
Vala	I told you he's only sticking around her because she's knocked up. If that ends, those feelings will be all mine.
Frazer	Then, why don't you take it now? You'll have Blake all to yourself. Go ahead, take it. What's wrong?

Vala	I guess I'm afraid.
Frazer	It doesn't hurt when you take it.
Vala	It's not that, I kind a wish it would.
Frazer	Then, what is your problem?
Vala	Do you think he'd really hate me?
Frazer	I think he'll feel betrayed.
Vala	I guess I should figure out better way.
Frazer	All right. I leave you alone.
Vala	Will you tell Dr. Skinner I didn't take it?
Frazer	Yes—I have to do my job.
Vala	What happens if I only take the first one and not the second?
Frazer	You'll make things even worse—you have to be absolutely committed either way.
Vala	All right.

He leaves her and meets Blake aside.

Blake	(With a plastic sack in hand) I have this for you.
Frazer	Good, I have to exam it right away.
Blake	Why, is something wrong?
Frazer	No, no. Everything's fine. I think you'd better talk with Vala over there; she needs to talk with you. Try to listen to her, will you?
Blake	I'll try.
Frazer	I mean it Blake, please, try to listen to her.

Frazer leaves them alone.

Scene 5

Blake   What did Skinner talk to you about after I left?

Vala   (Evasive) We talked about us.

Blake   (Desperate) What about us?

Vala   Take it easy, will yeah.

Blake   No, tell me.

Vala   No. First I want to know why you didn't tell me about the baby being screwed up?

Blake   It's none of your business.

Vala   Yes it is. You just don't trust me—that's all.

Blake   It's not your child; it's ours.

Vala   It's my fucking body too.

Blake   But it's our child.

Vala   You only want it 'cause she does.

Blake   That's not so.

Vala   How in the hell would you take care of it—let alone yourself?

Blake   I know it's going to be difficult, but we can make it. Help us?

Vala   No, everything will be much easier for us here.

Blake   Sandra disagrees; she wants the child, no matter what.

Vala   But if we keep the damn thing, Skinner will get rid of us.

Blake   So what, then let's leave.

Vala   No, who would help us?

Blake	We'd help each other.
Vala	But Skinner told me that we'll get no help outside of here, at least we can be helped here, please stay, please?
Blake	No. I'm leaving with her.
Vala	It won't work.
Blake	We can always come back if it doesn't.
Vala	Why are you so set on leaving, what the hell can you have out there, that you can't get here?
Blake	A family.
Vala	But what if she agreed to get rid of it and stay here?
Blake	I'd stay, but we're leaving once Frazer has found out how to help her...
Vala	Help her do what?
Blake	(Lying) She's wants to know more about the baby.
Vala	She already knows—Dr Skinner told me so.
Blake	Oh come on, he's lying to keep you here.
Vala	He's not! If my plan had worked, there would be no screwed up baby.
Blake	If your trap had worked the way you wanted it to, we'd be in the same situation anyway.
Vala	Not so! (Shows him a condom) I have this with me all the time, and I was going to give it to you.
Blake	You planned it well, didn't you. May be you screwed all this up. (Somewhat violent) You drugged me, you lured me into your room, and you tricked me into taking off all my clothes.

Vala	Because I love you, why can't you believe me?
Blake	Why do you love me?
Vala	I don't why. But ever since you two slept together, something inside of me keeps telling me I do and I can't get rid of it. Trust me, I tried to convince myself that I was not in love with you, but that feeling keeps stopping me. I've never felt this way before. But I am alone when this feeling happens to me. I guess that's why I want to be with you.
Blake	If you love me, keep the baby, that's all I got to say (Goes to leave).
Vala	Wait. I don't want to live with that feeling anymore unless your there.
Blake	You can have it if you help us. We could work it out. I don't know how we'd do it, but I'll try.
Vala	So, you do love me...you just have been afraid to tell me, that's all?
Blake	But I want you and Sandra all in one piece.
Vala	But not just me.
Blake	No.
Vala	They could help me get rid of her eventually...
Blake	No Fraz won't do that...he promised her...
Vala	I get it now, you're waiting for him to find a way to get rid of me.
Blake	(Silent).
Vala	You fucking assholes! Forget about your fucking family.
Blake	You won't stop us.

Vala	I will now (Taking out the RU-486) He told me if I take this there will be no more problems between us. You'll have to stay.
Blake	You can't force us to stay here.
Vala	I'm doing this for your own good.
Blake	No, you're not. We need to have the child. Don't take it away from us.
Vala	I'll do it because I love you.
Blake	Give it to me, I won't let you.

He wrestles her to the ground then pins her down.

Vala	Get off of me.
Blake	You little bitch!
Vala	Stop that, stop it! I'm not giving it to you. If Sandra could see now. She'd change her mind.

Blake stops in shock. She runs off.

Blake	Sandra! I didn't mean to…Sandra, where are you? I need you now.

He leaves quickly. Vala reappears shortly after, then she opens the package. She takes all of the RU-486 then throws the empty package to the ground, then runs off.

Scene 6

Dr Skinner is sitting at the computer examining Blake's gene print that Frazer gave him earlier.

Skin.   Did you destroy Blake's sperm sample?

Frazer   Yes, about an hour ago.

Skin.   Have you seen him since?

Frazer   No.

Skin.   Is the device ready?

Frazer   No, not yet.

Skin.   Why not?

Frazer   First, I want to know if you've finished the diagnosis of Blake's DNA print?

Skin.   Yes I have.

Frazer   (Waiting) So, what did you discover?

Skin.   You needn't worry about that now. You should be concerned with setting up the device.

Frazer   But I'd like to know, if you don't mind, or did you perform it at all?

Skin.   I performed it Mr. Frazer.

Frazer   Well then, what do you think led to the mutation?

Skin.   You're acting somewhat unprofessional, I think.

Frazer   I don't think so. I'm just trying to get to the facts—that's all. The results should be shared with me too. Isn't that professional?

Skin.   You're an intern here, and if you persist to question my authority, you are in jeopardy of losing that.

Frazer   I'm not questioning your authority, Dr. Skinner. I'm trying to find out the cause of Blake's problem. If we do, perhaps, we can still help them.

Skin.   Leave them alone. Just carry out my order!

Frazer   Before I consider that, I want to know how Blake was created?

Skin.   That's confidential.

Frazer   It must have been you?

Skin.   How do you figure that?

Frazer   I've read his dossier, and noticed your background is too similar to one of his donors. You're his father, aren't you? (No answer from Dr. Skinner) I am sure there are enough DNA samples around here that I can use to compare to his if I want to...

Skin.   Biologically yes. But Blake must never know that. I have a right to that confidentiality.

Frazer   I'll think about that. But you'd better tell me what caused the mutation.

Skin.   When I was an internship, like you, I discovered an anti-death gene that had a duplicating property in one of my earlier animal cases. It acted as an anti-body against disease.

Frazer   How so?

Skin.   It slows down the life span of a living gene when synthesized with the body. Essentially, the body's organisms live longer. I fused it to the genes of rats, first, and it progressed well.

Frazer   So, you had to try it out on a human being?

Skin.   It was inevitable. I extracted my sperm and fused it with a donor ovum. Then, I set out to fuse the anti-death gene with an embryo later on in its development.

Frazer You mean Blake?

Skin.   Not at first, it took a couple of tries before I had a viable embryo.

Frazer That's was Blake?

Skin.   Right. I thought once I introduced the anti-death gene into Blake's anti-bodies, his body's aging mechanism would be slowly demobilized.

Frazer (Fascinated) But how did you synthesize the anti-death gene to Blake's anti-bodies?

Skin.   I synthesized the anti-death gene with a virus. I knew the virus would naturally be attacked by his anti-bodies, and could be absorbed by them. It worked, and the anti-death gene had a domino effect inside his anti-bodies too. It was a marvelous thing to observe!

Frazer You mean the anti-death gene was to have a multiple effect on his antibodies?

Skin.   Yes, so numerous anti-death genes would duplicate within his anti-bodies, thus increase the life span of his anti-bodies and enable him to fight off diseases much more readily.

Frazer (Amazed) And increase his life span.

Skin.   Correct!

Frazer You're very proud of what you done, aren't you?

Skin.   I am. Theoretically, I am.

Frazer (Fascinated) Theoretically, it sounds like you were headed in the right direction.

Skin.   I thought I was.

Frazer   But what went wrong?

Skin.   The virus. It was only supposed to be a vehicle to carry the anti-death gene to the antibodies, and Blake's anti-bodies were supposed to kill it off.

Frazer   But they didn't.

Skin.   No.

Frazer   Instead—it caused the mutation.

Skin.   Yes.

Frazer   But how did it mutate?

Skin.   Mutations are not only unpredictable, but they inexplicable in terms of the environment. In that way they are very human. I guess what I am really saying is—I didn't know it did, until you gave me his gene print. When I examined it earlier, I observed that the virus had duplicated instead.

Frazer   So why did you notice now, and not earlier in his life?

Skin.   Technology! The technology! Back then I didn't have the equipment you have now. I didn't have the capability to enhance the lining as you do now. But when I magnified the one on the disk that you gave me, I recognized it was hidden within the synthetic lining. I've never seen it there before. That's the truth.

Frazer   Can we reverse the process somehow?

Skin.   No. Because there are unnatural stages at work now, and I am no longer able to reverse them.

Frazer   Can we do any further genetic manipulation that would help him?

Skin.   I'm not sure. If I had recognized the mutation a few years ago, then it might have been possible to correct.

Frazer   So his antibodies might not be able to fight off even a flu?

Skin.   That's correct, unfortunately.

Frazer   But, you said we could have helped him at an earlier stage?

Skin.   Yes, but, we can't reverse his life.

Frazer   No. I mean his child. If we stop Vala from taking the RU-486, at least we can help his child.

Skin.   (Very quiet)

Frazer   (Getting angry) Did you hear me?

Skin.   It's too late. She's probably taken it by now. (Frazer gets up to leave) Sit down, it's no use to try that now.

Frazer   My God. We must try.

Skin.   It should have worked.

Frazer   But it didn't!

Skin.   Sacrifices have to be made so it can be achieved one day. Don't you understand that?

Frazer   But isn't it wrong to intervene into the natural process?

Skin.   But we have the technology now. Sure, we'll make mistakes, but we can learn from them. This is a new era, never before has science been able to create. Just imagine if it had worked perfectly? His life span would have been increased, so much more.

Frazer   Yes, beyond that of Sandra and his child too.

Skin.	So, we'll make adjustments as we go along.
Frazer	And you don't mind playing God do you?
Skin.	Scientist do not believe in God Mr. Frazer, you must learn that very quickly. (Frazer gets up to leave again) I'm not finished yet.
Frazer	We might be able to stop Vala.
Skin.	You won't pursue that plan. What you will do is assist Blake to end his suffering.
Frazer	I will not!
Skin.	That would mean your intern here is incomplete and a bad evaluation. You should prepare to leave, now!
Frazer	I've had enough of you.

> *They exit.*

Scene 7

> *Sandra arrives all alone.*

Sandra	(Convulsing) Oh God, help me. Ah.
Blake	(He enters unnoticed and grabs her) Where is it? I want it—give it to me.
Sandra	(Screams) Blake stop it—you're hurting me!
Blake	Tell me what did with it?
Sandra	Blake it's me, Sandra. Please stop it—that hurts. Let go of me.
Blake	Sandra...I thought it was Vala.
Sandra	Yes. It's me.
Blake	Oh God, I'm sorry.
Sandra	(Looking at his bear arm) What happened here?

Blake	I'm not sure. But there's a lot more of it now, and the bumps are getting bigger.
Sandra	We've got to get you help—soon.
Blake	Have you found a small package on you?
Sandra	No.
Blake	Look, then.
Sandra	(She checks her pockets) Nothing. Why?
Blake	Skinner gave Vala the medication.
Sandra	Oh, God, I don't want to hear that.
Blake	I hope it's not too late. How are you feeling?
Sandra	I vomited earlier and my stomach is still sore. But maybe it's just the alcohol she drank. Didn't you try to stop her?
Blake	Yes, but she ran off before I could take it from her.
Sandra	(crying) Please tell me she didn't take it.

> *She finds the empty package that Vala threw on the ground earlier.*

Blake	That' it!
Sandra	It's empty! (She throws the package away) God, I feel empty! Oh, God, I'm going to puke.

> *She wants to vomit but can't. Vala appears and looks at Blake with fright, then goes to run, but stops all of a sudden.*

Blake	Where are you going Sandra? (She stops) Are you okay?
Vala	Where am I?
Blake	Sandra?

Vala   Yes. It's me Blake. I'm sorry, I forgot. What did you say?

Blake   I said she ran off before I could get the drug from her.

Vala   (She feels pain again) Do you know how it is to feel sick and alone. Blake, hold me?

Blake   But I should go find Frazer.

Vala   I don't care about that. I feel sick, help me, please. Just take me, would you. Please, please, hold me.

Blake   All right.

Vala   (When he takes her closer she sees the rash) What are these?

Blake   (Aware that it may be Vala) You know what they are? I just told you.

Vala   Oh, yah. I am just feeling out of it. I forgot, that's all.

Blake   (Knowing that it is Vala) Sandra, why can't we get rid of the child?

Vala   (She is somewhat aware of Blake's change in attitude) Because, we should keep together.

Blake   But don't you think we'd be really killing it?

Vala   I'm not sure what you're getting at.

Blake   You don't think it would be morally wrong to (With emphasis) dispose of it.

Vala   I don't even know why you're bringing this up now.

Blake   And you don't mind me saying 'dispose'?

Vala   (Silence).

Blake	(Standing and more aggressive) You don't think I know who I'm talking to?
Vala	(Holding her down) Blake, stop it! How come you're treating me like this?
Blake	You think you've deceived me again, but I know who you are. Where's the rest of the medication, I want it now. Give it to me.
Vala	(Faking Sandra) Blake it's me Sandra, please believe me. (He grabs her) Stop it, stop it. You're acting like Skinner said you would.
Blake	Tell me, where is it, give it to me—now!
Vala	I don't have it. You're hurting me—let go!
Blake	(Holding her tighter) You are killing our child!
Vala	(Breaking away from him) Yes, I swallowed the whole fucking thing. You have no damn kid now, because it's going to burn in hell. Just the way the fucking world ends...Oh God. I'm sick. I feel really sick Blake, go get Skinner, please, go get someone.

She appears to look drowsy.

Blake	(He begins to force her to vomit by squeezing her stomach) You'll puke it out whether you like it or not.
Vala	Blake stop it, you're hurting me. Stop fucking grabbing me!
Blake	Puke it now! Puke it out! Puke it—now!
Vala	(She is fighting with him now) You want it, you can fucking have it. (She spits in his face)
	(Grabbing at him as he leaves her) No, don't Blake.

She begins to vomit on the floor, then passes out.

Blake	(Going to her) Sandra? Sandra, do you hear me? I'll go get help. (Turning to leave when he sees Frazer) Fraz, you got to help, help her!
Frazer	What happened? (Frazer checks her pulse).
Blake	I tried to force her to vomit.
Frazer	You forced her to do what?
Blake	No, you don't understand. She took all the medication, all of it; she told me!
Frazer	I told Dr. Skinner not to give it all to her. Damn!
Blake	So you didn't give it to her?
Frazer	No. Can you hear me Sandra? Sandra talk to us. Blake's here too.
Blake	It's Vala, not Sandra!
Frazer	She nodded a bit, I think. Let's move her so she can breathe easier.

As they are moving her, she violently screams.

Blake	There's blood!
Frazer	She's hemorrhaging. (He moves her onto her side) There she's breathing better. She's coming to. (Angry) She wasn't supposed to take the whole damn thing at once!
Blake	We've lost our baby—Sandra—it's gone.
Frazer	Sandra—can you hear me?
Blake	This will kill her; it's all my fault.
Frazer	No it isn't.
Blake	But Vala took it because of me.
Fraz.	No. Dr. Skinner gave it all to her to cover up his mess.

86

Blake	What are you talking about?
Fraz.	He caused the mutation in your baby...
Skin.	(Skinner arrives) I want to know who took all the methadone from my office?
Frazer	Vala!
Skin.	What's happening here?
Frazer	She took all of the medication.
Skin	All of it.
Frazer	You gave it all to her?
Skin.	I did, but I told her not to take all of it at the same time.
Frazer	You're lying! (Turning to Blake) I guess it's about time for the truth.
Blake	About what?
Frazer	(addressing Dr. Skinner) You should tell him.
Skin.	Tell him what?
Frazer	If you don't—I will.
Skin.	You keep this confidential, Mr. Frazer, or else... ·
Frazer	I'm sick of lying for you. Tell him now!
Skin.	(Waiting somewhat, looking at Frazer then back to Blake) I created you.
Blake	You created me?
Skin.	I am your donor.
Blake	You're my father?
Skin.	Biologically, yes.
Frazer	That's not all of it, what about the mutation? He has every right to know.

Skin. All right.

Blake Know what?

Skin. I caused your mutation when I fused an alien gene to your antibodies.

Blake Alien gene...the rash on my arms?

Skin. Yes. But, I didn't intend it to turn out this way.

Blake (Angrily) The mutation in our child too...

Skin. (Silent)

Blake (He attacks Skinner) You...

Frazer Let him go Blake.

Skin. Take your hands off me. Listen to me...Listen to me. I created you!

Blake (Putting his hands around Skinner's neck and squeezing them together) You're not leaving Walden now!

Frazer Stop it now Blake! Don't do it!

Skin. I can't breathe, let me go. Help Mr. Frazer...Help...

Blake You're going to burn in hell too!

Frazer If you take his life, you'll be just like him!

Sandra Blake—leave him alone—we've had enough of him.

Sandra seeing the blood on her, she violently cries.

Blake (Running to her) Sandra? It could be Vala, Fraz?

Sandra She's gone. I can feel it. She's gone.

Blake The baby's gone?

Sandra   No. Vala's gone. I heard a scream, her voice for the first time. I felt her leave. She's gone. Do you hear me? She's gone! We can have our child now Blake; she can't stop us now.

Silence among them all.

Frazer   Sandra...Vala took all the medication, before we could stop her, that's why you've hemorrhaged. I'm sorry. I'm really sorry.

Sandra cries softly, then is silent.

Blake   (He goes to attack Skinner again). You'll pay for what you did to her...

Skin.   Not me—Vala!

Frazer attempts to stop Blake.

Blake   Then you can join her...

Skin.   Sandra, stop him...Sandra, please?

Sandra   Blake...If you love me—stop now!

Blake releases Dr. Skinner.

Sandra   We've had enough. Let's leave—now! We'll leave together.

Frazer   Sandra—you're too weak to walk.

Skin.   You won't survive out there.

Blake   We'll make it fine—without you. Sandra, I'm ready to leave with you now.

Sandra   Help me then.

They exit.

Frazer   (He takes off his white coat and throws it to Skinner) I've had enough you too. I'm leaving. (Turning to Blake and Sandra) Blake, Sandra, wait for me.

Skin.   You'll lose everything. Everything. Everyone. It's so unpredictable. Mutations.

> *He exits, leaving Dr. Skinner alone on stage. The lights dim and darkness encloses Skinner while the following telephone recorded message is heard in the voice of Frazer:*

Welcome to our human enrichment center at Walden. If you are interested in any of our genetic counseling programs, please leave your name and number after the tone, and we will contact you as soon as possible. Thank you.

> *In the voice of a female:*

Hello, Oh, I heard about your genetic enrichment program, and I'm very interesting in participating in it before having a child. My number is 555-1212, okay. Thank you. Oh, I forgot, it's Mary Joseph.

THE END

ABOUT THE AUTHOR

Gilbert McInnis has earned his Ph.D in English Literature at Université Laval. He recently published a monograph, *Evolutionary Mythology in the Writings of Kurt Vonnegut* (2011). He has contributed an Introduction to a new release of Paul Goodman's *Moral Ambiguity of America*, acted as editor for a debut work by the American poet Erik Wackernagel's *She Bang Slam* and Sir Leonard Woolley's *Ur of Chaldees*. He taught English literature at Université Laval, Université Chicoutimi and Bishop's University in Québec, at Grenfell College in Newfoundland, and at Acadia University in Nova Scotia. He currently serves as Senior Writing Tutor for Dalhousie University, Halifax.

www.ingramcontent.com/pod-product-compliance
Lightning Source LLC
LaVergne TN
LVHW041231080426
835508LV00011B/1163